BRITAIN IN OLD PHOTOGRAPHS

THE LONDON BOROUGH OF
WALTHAM FOREST

NIGEL SADLER

SUTTON PUBLISHING LIMITED

Sutton Publishing Limited
Phoenix Mill · Thrupp · Stroud
Gloucestershire · GL5 2BU

First published 1998

Cover photographs: *Front*: Councillor Golightly
laying foundation stone for the Lea Bridge
Road Library, 1905. *Back*: the grocer J.E. Ball
with his horse Rufus, Walthamstow, *c*. 1895.
Title page: Mr Frank Duggan, the driver of
Leyton libraries van, loading new books for
Whipps Cross Hospital, 1952.

British Library Cataloguing in Publication Data
A catalogue record for this book is available from the
British Library.

ISBN 0-7509-1738-5

Typeset in 10/12 Perpetua.
Typesetting and origination by
Sutton Publishing Limited.
Printed in Great Britain by
Ebenezer Baylis, Worcester.

Upper Walthamstow Road, Walthamstow, *c*. 1910.

CONTENTS

The interior of the barn at Pimp Hall Farm, Chingford, *c.* 1900. This seventeenth-century building was blown down in 1990 after many years of neglect had weakened it. Unfortunately, its collapse coincided with a project to restore it.

INTRODUCTION

The London Borough of Waltham Forest began life in 1965 with the amalgamation of the boroughs of Chingford, Leyton and Walthamstow. Originally part of Essex, the area was primarily agricultural up until the late Victorian times when the arrival of the railways and sales of the large farm and private estates to developers prompted rapid growth. Between 1851 and 1991 the population of the area covered by modern day Waltham Forest rose from around 10,000 to over 210,000.

Archaeological work has shed a little light on the earlier populations of the area. Flint tools have been found and remains of mammoth, bison, reindeer and wild pig suggest that the area supported an active hunter-gatherer Stone Age society. Evidence indicates that there were small villages along the River Lea and from the Iron Age some remains have been found of pile villages, that is houses built on platforms above the flood plain. It is possible that the name Chingford derives from Caegingaford, or the ford of the dwellers of the stumps.

For the Roman period little *in situ* evidence has been found but it is clear Roman roads crossed this area. By Saxon times several villages had been founded and in Walthamstow these included Church End, Higham Hill, Wood Street and Hale End. It is at this stage that Walthamstow and Leyton gained their names; Walthamstow is derived from Wilcumestow, a place of welcome, which was one of the two local manors in modern day Walthamstow while Leyton gained its name from tun or settlement by the River Lea.

During the medieval period manors and parishes developed throughout the area and many of the large estates and churches were founded. The latter included the parish churches of All Saints, Chingford, St Mary's, Walthamstow, and St Mary's, Leyton. By the Tudor period rich merchant families from the City had started to move into the area and this trend continued in the seventeenth and eighteenth centuries when farming became the major source of income for the district; small industries such as brick and tile making had also begun by this time and mills had been founded along the River Lea.

But it was in the nineteenth century that the greatest changes were to occur. The railway station at Lea Bridge opened in 1840 and common land started to be enclosed. In 1870 the Great Eastern Railway opened a branch to Shernhall Street (now Wood Street) and offered cheap labourers' fares to encourage use. The large estates of Leyton and Walthamstow were sold off for housing development and by the end of the nineteenth century there was an uncomfortable relationship between the traditional farming that had been dominant in the area and the threats presented by ever-expanding housing and industrial development.

The twentieth century saw a rapid increase in industry and the end of agriculture in the area, with the last farm closing in 1952. There were also major changes in transport with horse-drawn vehicles making way for electric trams and petrol/diesel driven vehicles. The streets designed for a low level of horse traffic are now congested by motor cars while the once proud avenues have either lost their trees or have poor examples of trees remaining. The open spaces have shrunk but in turn leisure facilities have been provided including parks, libraries, museums, swimming baths, leisure centres, cinemas and theatres.

However as Leyton and then Walthamstow grew rapidly, Chingford remained less developed, partly because the cheap workers' train fares were not extended beyond Higham's Park Station but also because landowners were less willing to sell off their land. It was not until the 1920s that some of the bigger estates in Chingford started to be developed but the Epping Forest Act of 1878 prevented building work moving northwards.

The Second World War forced changes in the borough. In the late 1940s planning departments came up with new housing, retail and manufacturing developments to rebuild the scarred streets. Some of these were implemented immediately – such as the temporary Nissen huts and prefabs – but it was not until the late 1950s and early 1960s that most of the large housing estates were begun. Like elsewhere in the country, the tower blocks rose and were seen as the solution to mass housing shortages. With hindsight we can now say that many failed to live up to the expectations and in the 1990s – some of these tower blocks have been demolished and more community-minded low-level housing constructed.

Since the 1950s the area covered by Waltham Forest today has become a popular place for many people who emigrated to Britain especially from the Caribbean, India and Pakistan. Now over a quarter of the population of Waltham Forest belongs to the ethnic communities and the borough has the second largest Pakistani population in Britain. This multicultural flavour makes Waltham Forest one of the most exciting places to live in London and and it has great potential for development in the near future.

The area has also had its fair share of resident celebrities. They include not only people with a local reputation such as George Monoux (1477–1544), Lord Mayor of London, but also those with international reputations including in Walthamstow, William Morris (1834–96), in Leyton, Alfred Hitchcock (1899–1980) and in Chingford, the Manchester United footballer David Beckham (born 1975). Also, who can forget the band East 17 who have made the Walthamstow postcode known throughout the world, as well as using Walthamstow as the name for their first album in 1992.

This book represents only a small part of the photographic archive of Vestry House Museum and includes previously unseen images where possible. Unfortunately, it reflects the history of collecting photographs in Chingford, Leyton and Walthamstow: the active library service in Leyton and the museum in Walthamstow meant that these parts of Waltham Forest were fairly well covered. Chingford did not have such an active library service and the responsibility for recording local history fell to the Chingford Historical Society, which was also hampered by the fact that the borough was less photographed. With the formation of Waltham Forest the Leyton and Walthamstow photographic archives were amalgamated, including a limited number of Chingford images. Added to these archives on loan was the limited number of images collected by the Chingford Historical Society. Vestry House Museum now collects for the whole of Waltham Forest and is trying to rectify this inequality of coverage.

CHAPTER ONE

POLITICS

Leyton town hall, High Road, decorated for the coronation of King George V, 1911. This building was designed by J. Johnson and built in 1896, replacing the first town hall built in 1882 which became the public library.

The first town hall for Walthamstow, Orford Road, September 1908. With the Public Health Act of 1872 the administration of the parish of Walthamstow was split between the Vestry and the Local Board. The Local Board still met at the Vestry on Vestry Road but in 1876 the Public Hall on Orford Road was extended to become the town hall.

Celebrations at Walthamstow town hall, Forest Road, possibly to mark the 1951 Festival of Britain. In 1941 Walthamstow Borough Council moved to its new town hall on Forest Road which was designed by P.D. Hepworth and in 1965 became the town hall for Waltham Forest.

Children playing at the Walthamstow town hall pond, 1954. A major summer attraction for local children was the town hall pond where they would paddle and play with their model boats. The pond is still there today.

Mr J.S. Johnson, the defeated Unionist candidate in Walthamstow, driving through the constituency in 1910.

In 1938 Chingford marked its Charter Day with a procession attended by the Lord Mayor of London and here his coach is pictured at the foot of Chingford Mount.

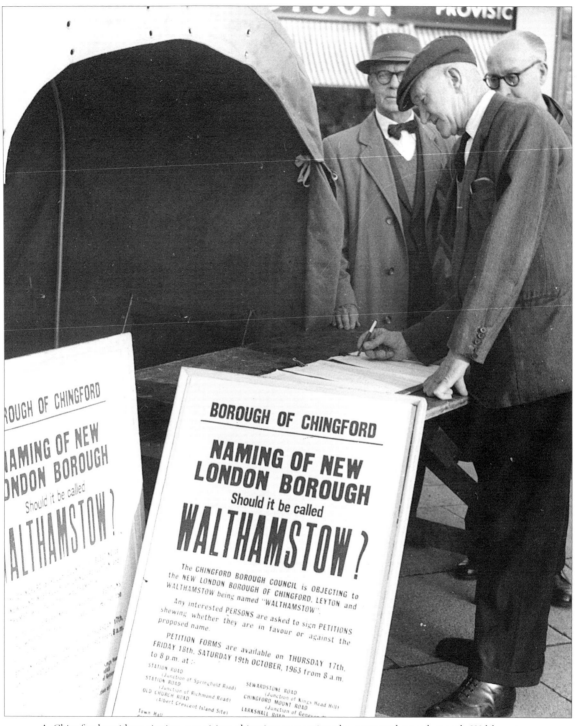

A Chingford resident signing a petition objecting to naming the proposed new borough Walthamstow, October 1963. In 1965 the former boroughs of Chingford, Leyton and Walthamstow combined to form the London Borough of Waltham Forest. Originally it had been suggested that the new borough be called Walthamstow but Leyton and Chingford Councils objected.

Visitors to the Leyton Borough Council's Town Planning Exhibition, February 1948. Immediately after the Second World War the boroughs of Chingford, Leyton and Walthamstow all had to undertake major redevelopment programmes to restore the war-scarred streets. Various exhibitions were held to keep the local residents informed of proposed developments.

Leyton Urban District Council's staff outing ready to depart from outside the town hall, High Road, Leyton, c. 1900. In late Victorian times many local companies adopted the practice of taking their staff on an annual outing and this also spread into local government.

CHAPTER TWO

RELIGION

St Mary's church, Walthamstow, 1908. St Mary's is the parish church for Walthamstow and it is probable that a church has occupied this site from Anglo-Saxon times. The first permanent building was constructed in the twelfth century and since then there have been many modifications, mostly dating from the eighteenth and nineteenth centuries. Today the paths around the church are used as short cuts by pedestrians and cyclists but there is nothing new in this as is shown by this image which displays a sign prohibiting cyclists.

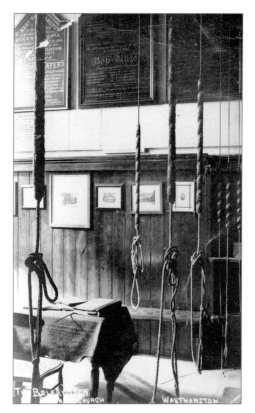

Interior of the bell tower, St Mary's church, Walthamstow, *c.* 1910. The bell tower has dominated the Walthamstow Village area ever since it was constructed in 1535 by George Monoux.

The bells of St Mary's church, Walthamstow, were removed in 1896 for an overhaul. Many locals came to view the spectacle.

All Saints' church, Chingford Mount, Chingford, *c.* 1910. There is mention of a church on this site in the twelfth century and All Saints' church is first mentioned in 1397. By 1710 it had become St Peter's and St Paul's but this title was transferred to the new parish church in 1844. It was renamed All Saints', colloquially known as Chingford old church, and slowly fell into disrepair.

Interior of Chingford old church, Chingford Mount Road, before the roof collapsed in 1904. If the church had not been restored through the generosity of Miss S.L. Boothby Heathcote in 1929 it would have been demolished.

St Peter's and St Paul's, Chingford Green, *c.* 1890. This church, designed by Lewis Vulliamy, became the parish church in 1844 and the twelfth-century font and eighteenth-century pulpit were transferred from the old parish church.

St Mary the Virgin, the parish church for Leyton, Church Road, May 1901. It was built in the seventeenth century, with major additions in the nineteenth century. In the 1930s the building underwent various alterations and extensions and in the 1990s a fire caused by vandals led to further restoration work.

St John the Baptist church, Church Lane, Leytonstone, *c.* 1898. This church has its origins in a smaller chapel built in 1749. In 1833 the present church was opened just north of the original chapel. St John's was enlarged in 1893 and 1910 to cater for the growing population and in 1956 the church was restored. It still dominates the corner of Church Road and the High Road, Leytonstone.

St George's Old Presbytery, Walthamstow, *c.* 1900. A small mission chapel dedicated to St George was opened in 1849 by Dr (later Cardinal) Nicholas Wiseman who was living at Shern Hall. In 1901 a massive brick building was opened, known as Our Lady and St George; it was burnt down on 2 April 1993 and rebuilt in 1996.

St Peter's in the Forest church on Woodford New Road, Walthamstow, *c.* 1910. Built in 1840, the church was extended in 1887 and was badly damaged by a V2 rocket in 1945; repairs were made in 1951.

Harvest Festival at All Saints' church, Capworth Street, Leyton, 1950s.

Many preachers did not require a building to pass on their messages. The annual rally of open-air preachers, shown here in 1924 as they passed Folkestone Road Evangelical church, allowed the placard-carrying speakers to pass on their teachings to the people of Walthamstow.

St Luke's church on Greenleaf Road, Walthamstow has its roots in a mission founded in 1900 and was built in 1902, probably the date of this photograph. The boy in the entrance is Cecil Charles Groome, the only child of Joseph Groome who was the first verger of St Luke's. Cecil died at Gaza in March 1917 aged twenty-six while fighting in the First World War.

CHAPTER THREE

EDUCATION

Pupils of Winns Avenue School queuing outside 556 Forest Road, Walthamstow, September 1945. One of the strangest incidents relating to education in Walthamstow happened in 1945 when sixty-five senior school children from Winns Avenue School went on strike against the Education Authority which had closed their school down. For eleven weeks they refused to go to their new schools and used a disused shop on Forest Road as a temporary classroom. Ultimately the strike failed.

Boys practising at Harrow Green School for the tug of war at school sports, July 1896. In Victorian times schools aimed to enhance children mentally and physically. A great believer in the importance of healthy children was the headteacher of Harrow Green School, A.P. Wire, who held sports competitions and encouraged staff to take pupils on walks in the nearby forest. Mr Wire was a prolific photographer and took many scenes of Essex as well as his school.

Girls drill at the school sports day in Leyton, 1902. Sports days played an important part in the life of schoolchildren and all were expected to take part even if it was just performing a drill.

The gym at Monoux Grammar School, Chingford Road, Walthamstow, 1930s. Pupils were expected to participate in sports outdoors and in the gym. The gym at Monoux Grammar School was probably better equipped than those at most other schools.

Boys of Leyton High Road School gardening, c. 1910. School was not only intended to provide education in the three Rs but also to provide moral welfare, fitness and a background in everyday skills, many of which would be used in the work young people would get when they left.

Church Road School orchestra, Leyton, 1930. Extra-curricula activities usually included sport and music; orchestras would rehearse after lessons and perform at school events.

The Greek Theatre at Walthamstow Girls' School, Church Hill, Walthamstow, 1930. Most schools had stages in their main hall for performances but the Girls' School went one stage further and using unemployed labour built an open-air theatre in its grounds. It was opened by Sybil Thorndike, who starred in the first performance, *Medea*, on 2 July 1925.

The 'Old Woman that Lived in a Shoe' tableau produced by Newport Junior School, Newport Road, Leyton, 1934. The shoe was made by the woodwork master at Newport Senior School for the opening of Leyton Baths, High Road, Leyton.

Children examining their packets of sweets after distribution from New Zealand at Coppermill Lane School, Walthamstow, 10 March 1950. At this date sweets were still on ration following the Second World War and were a luxury for many children.

Pupils from the School of Dancing, Rectory Road, Walthamstow, 1931. The classes were run by Mrs Collins who taught elocution, recitation and scenarios. Schools similar to this provided an important role especially for children whose schools failed to provide sufficient activities.

Pupils from the Chingford National School dressed as playing cards on Chingford Plain, 1927.

Laying of the foundation stone at St Joseph's Roman Catholic School, Leyton, 12 May 1900. With the increasing population at the end of the Victorian era more schools were needed. The upper floor of this school housed the church until 1904.

Capworth Street School, Leyton, *c.* 1900. Originally it was felt inappropriate to educate boys and girls in the same class or even in the same school. Schools therefore had separate entrances for boys and girls and this image shows the boys' school on the left and girls' school on the right.

Ruckholt Lane Board School, Ruckholt Lane, Leyton shows the cookery class run by Miss Tyres, 1896. Schools were sexist in what and how they taught. It was assumed that girls would become mothers and homemakers which meant their education was directed this way.

Cookery class at Sidney Burnell School, Handsworth Avenue, Walthamstow, 1969. Educational sexism lasted well into the twentieth century as is illustrated by this cookery class but more recently schools have tried to steer away from the stereotypical classes for boys and girls.

Wood workshop at Norlington County Secondary Modern School, Norlington Road, Leyton, 1964. Boys were expected to carry out lessons in skills that could be transferred to the workplace, including wood and metalworking, and were also encouraged to be competitive through sports.

Pretoria Avenue school stores, Walthamstow, 1947. With so many schools in Walthamstow the education department had to have large food stores and from the food visible we can surmise that the schoolchildren were well fed. It was also possible that these stores may have supplied other venues as rationing was still in place.

Mr Waterman, the caretaker at Thomas Gamuel School, with the coke cart for the school fires, *c.* 1920.
He was also gardener for St Mary's church, Walthamstow.

CHAPTER FOUR

TRANSPORT

A coach outside the Three Blackbirds pub, High Road, Leyton, is about to set off on a day's outing,
c. 1890. Before the railways, horse-drawn coaches were the dominant form of public transport. However,
even after trains were introduced, horse-drawn coaches were still commonly used for day trips by local groups.
It was not until the development of the charabancs at the beginning of the twentieth century that horses
ceased to be used.

A horse-drawn tram outside the West Ham Union Workhouse, Union Road (now Langthorne Road), Leytonstone, 1890s. For public road transport the horse and coach was initially replaced by horse-drawn trams which operated along Lea Bridge Road, Leyton and High Road, Leytonstone, to Whipps Cross between 1883 and 1905.

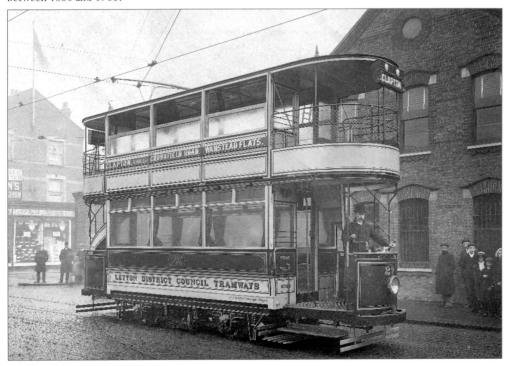

A Leyton tram on its route to Clapton, c. 1910. Walthamstow and Leyton Urban District Councils decided to run their own tram services. Leyton purchased the existing local horse drawn tram companies and came to an agreement with Walthamstow and Hackney into whose boroughs these services ran.

Laying of tramlines at the junction of Whipps Cross Road and Lea Bridge Road, 1906. Laying of these lines caused major disruption to roads, a still continuing theme in Leyton and Leytonstone with the development of the M11 link road today. The old horse trough is being used as a seat by a workman.

To provide shelter from the elements the Leyton Urban District Council constructed a large depot on Lea Bridge Road in 1906.

The Walthamstow Urban District Council tram depot on Chingford Road, *c.* 1910. During the 1990s the sheds were demolished; and the land and the offices were developed into housing.

The yard of the tram depot, Chingford Road, Walthamstow, *c.* 1935. In 1933 Walthamstow buses and trams were taken over by London Passenger Transport Board.

An AEC B-type bus in service in Leyton with adverts for Warner Estates property, *c.* 1916. Trams were soon to meet competition from the developing bus services. The local company, Associated Equipment Company (AEC), played a major part in this change of public transport as it designed and manufactured the B-type which became the dominant bus on the roads between 1910 and 1920.

Chingford Hatch level-crossing, *c.* 1905. Initially the railway line between Liverpool Street and Chingford ended its journey in a fairly rural area. There was no problem with excessive traffic trying to cross the lines so in certain areas the railway was only guarded by a level crossing. Today, however, this crossing becomes congested when trains arrive at or depart from Higham's Park station.

Hoe Street station, Walthamstow, *c.* 1870. The Great Eastern line was extended into Walthamstow with the opening of Hoe Street station on 26th April 1870.

The rear entrance to Hoe Street station, *c.* 1913. This area now comprises a picking up point, a taxi waiting area and a car park for rail users.

Chingford station opened in 1873 and encouraged daytrippers to visit the forest. Despite the coming of the railway and development that followed, Chingford remained a rural area well up until the First World War. The main reason for this was that the railway companies did not extend the cheap workmen's fares beyond Higham's Park which also accounts for the grander houses.

In 1911 there was a railway strike and soldiers were drafted in to protect railway stations and goods yards. Here soldiers are seen resting at Temple Mills, Leyton.

A 661 trolleybus on the High Road, Leytonstone, near the junction with Gainsborough Road, 1959. In 1936/7 trams were replaced by trolleybuses with tramlines either being dug up or buried under new road surfaces. On 18 August 1959 trolleybus 661 was replaced by bus route 26 and by 1960 all trolleybus services had been replaced.

Buses pulling up outside Leyton Underground station, High Road, Leyton, 1964. The underground system entered the area with the opening of the Central Line stations between Stratford and Leytonstone in May 1947. While the station and road have changed very little, the M11 extension being constructed during the 1990s has had a major impact on surrounding streets, housing and shops.

It was the responsibility of the councils to build and maintain roads and to do this they purchased specialist vehicles. In about 1950 a Walthamstow Borough Council roadroller ran out of control at the waterworks, Forest Road, and eventually crashed in Albion Road slightly injuring the driver.

The councils also owned a wide range of other vehicles. In 1916 Walthamstow Urban District Council purchased one of the first steam-driven water wagons.

During 1963 boreholes were made in the borough, like the one in First Avenue, Walthamstow (above), to see how suitable the land was for the development of the underground into the area. The Victoria Line between Seven Sisters and Walthamstow, including Blackhorse Lane, opened on 1 September 1968.

CHAPTER FIVE

PUBLIC SERVICES
& UTILITIES

Laying the gas mains at the Baker's Arms, Leyton, 1901. Gas was not only supplied to houses for lighting, heating and cooking, it also provided fuel for the street lamps, an ever-increasing demand as road traffic grew.

View of the Lea Bridge Gasworks, Lea Bridge Road, Leyton, 4 January 1923. These gasworks were built in 1853 by the South Essex Gaslight and Coke Company which was bought out by the Lea Bridge District Gaslight and Coke Company in 1868. In 1878 it reincorporated as Lea Bridge District Gas Company and after the Gas Act of 1948 both companies were transferred to the North Thames gas board.

The Exeter Road Power Station, Walthamstow, 1960s. The power station opened in September 1901 and was located near to the railways for a ready supply of coal. It was known by its distinctive chimneys, and ceased generating electricity in about 1960 but did not close until March 1968.

The local councils had many duties from the outset, most of which are still carried out today. This steam-driven refuse collector was the property of Walthamstow Urban District Council in about 1920. The bucket on the back carried disinfectant that was put into dustbins.

The Auckland Road Depot, Leyton, 1962. After many complaints relating to sewage, works were opened in Auckland Road in 1883. The accumulation of residual sludge led to the construction of a destructor at the site in 1896 which was also used for burning houschold refuse until about 1962 when the council agreed to bulk disposal of refuse after salvage by tipping outside the borough.

North Metropolitan Fire Brigade at Whipps Cross, Leytonstone, *c.* 1879. Formed in 1865, the fire service was run by volunteers and funded through the local board and subscriptions. In 1903 the first paid fireman was employed by Leyton UDC.

Forest Road fire station, Walthamstow, 1894. The demands of an ever increasing population meant that there was a need for a more organised and better equipped fire service. The response to the need is illustrated by the assorted equipment shown here.

Chingford police station, Kings Head Hill, 1900. With the increasing population, law and order became of prime concern and it was maintained in rural Chingford from this small police station, built in 1887; in 1977 a purpose-built station was constructed.

Walthamstow police station, Forest Road, *c.* 1905. In the faster developing Walthamstow the police station was much larger. The original Metropolitan police station was at the present site of Vestry House Museum and after moving to Lea Bridge Road in 1870, it moved to Forest Road in 1892.

Leytonstone police station, High Road, Leytonstone, *c.* 1913. Alfred Hitchcock, who was born just up the road in 1899, recalled the time he was sent as a five year old to the police station with a note. Upon reading the note the policeman locked young Alfred in the cell stating 'this is what we do to naughty boys'. This memory lasted with Alfred Hitchcock all his life and in his films wrongful imprisonment or accusations played a large part.

Emergency feeding exercise outside Leyton town hall, 12 October 1954. The local authorities also maintained civil defence units and in Leyton Jenny Hammond was the Civil Defence Co-ordinator, shown in the dark uniform pointing left. The men in hats are Mr Coates, London Region Officer (left) and Mr Warden the Regional Food Emergency Officer (right).

A ward at the Cottage Hospital, Salisbury Road, Walthamstow, 1880s. Healthcare for local residents has been provided by several hospitals: the original was a voluntary institution founded in 1877/8 on Brandon Road, off Wood Street. In 1880 it moved to Salisbury Road, where it remained until 1894 when it was transferred to Holmcroft, Orford Road. In 1928 it was renamed the Connaught Hospital after its patron the Duchess of Connaught and closed in 1980.

Whipps Cross Hospital, Whipps Cross Road, Leyton, *c*. 1910. This is the most famous of the local hospitals. The house and land of Forest House were purchased in 1889 by the West Ham guardians and an infirmary opened in 1903; the impressive front quickly became a local landmark.

A branch of the Brentwood Lunatic Asylum at the Chestnuts, Hoe Street, Walthamstow, *c*. 1907. Originally built as a large private house in about 1745, it became a branch of the Brentwood Lunatic Asylum. Then in 1919 it was taken over as a commercial and trade school for girls which became part of the South West Essex Technical College and moved to Forest Road, Walthamstow, in 1938. Chestnuts continued to be used for evening classes and until 1957 housed the overflow of college students. Today it is the offices of the London Borough of Waltham Forest Education Department.

St Mary's Orphanage, *c.* 1910. Walthamstow House, Shernall Street, was built in about 1772 and was once the home of the Wigram family (1782–1842). The house became a preparatory school for boys between 1842 and 1860, by 1882 it was home to a Roman Catholic Poor Law school for girls and in 1901 it housed 170 girls and was called St Mary's Orphanage. It ceased to be a school in 1931 but remained a convent and children's home until 1983. In 1986 Corpus Christi Catholic High School moved into the premises.

As the community developed the post office had to grow too. The sorting offices, such as this one in Church Lane, Leyton, *c.* 1905, were built and then extended while the number of postmen employed rose sharply.

The West Ham Union Board of Guardians at the presentation to Miss Duncan, the retiring chair, April 1914. For the poor of the area the workhouse provided shelter and food in return for work. In 1834 the West Ham Poor Law Union was formed and included Walthamstow, Leyton and various other neighbouring parishes. Inmates from the Walthamstow and Leyton workhouses were transferred in 1840 to the newly built West Ham Union, now Langthorne Hospital.

The parish-run Leyton Almshouse, Church Road, 1901. Prior to the welfare state it was the parish, individual benefactors, companies or cooperatives that had to look after people who had fallen on hard times. The most common forms of help were the workhouse or almshouse.

The Monoux Almshouses, 1903. The almshouses, with the associated school and feast hall for the poor of Walthamstow, were built in 1527 by George Monoux, alderman of London and local worthy. The school was based here for 353 years before moving to the High Street, Walthamstow. The western end of Monoux's building was reconstructed in 1955 after being hit by a high explosive bomb in 1940.

The London Master Bakers' Benevolent Institution, better known as Baker's Almshouse, Lea Bridge Road, Leyton, c. 1930. The master bakers built this almshouse between 1857 and 1866 as housing for members who had fallen on hard times.

A flooded Lea Bridge Road, Leyton, July 1949. Because the River Lea forms the borough's western boundary this area has undergone flooding throughout history. The major flood of 1947 led to prevention plans being formulated but even after these the river continued to burst its banks.

Leyton residents collecting water in 1947. In times of flooding various facilities were put out of operation. During the 1947 flood this included the pumping station on Lea Bridge Road and local residents had to be supplied with an alternative source of water.

CHAPTER SIX

HOUSING

The estate offices for O.H. Watling, just prior to the building of Beech Hall Road, c. 1904. It is claimed that the Regal cinema was built on the site of this office.

Houses built by the Warner Estate on Carr Road, looking towards Winns Avenue, Walthamstow, *c.* 1905.
The largest development in Walthamstow was the Warner estate. The company left its mark on the
evolution of the area with its distinctive houses where the wood was painted cream and green.

The Warner Estate was clearly well versed in marketing its properties either for sale or rent and produced a
series of interior photographs such as this one of the drawing-room in a cottage on Bemstead Road, *c.* 1905.

The Ancient House, Walthamstow, 1908. This fifteenth- or sixteenth-century timber-framed and wattle and daub structure had shops added to the ground floor in the nineteenth century.

In 1934 the owners of the Ancient House, Fullers the Builders, carried out an extensive restoration of the building as a memorial to the late W.G. Fuller.

Queen Elizabeth's Hunting Lodge, Ranger's Road, Chingford, *c.* 1910. This building is misnamed: it was originally built by Henry VIII in 1543 as a grandstand from which hunts could be viewed and past which deer could be driven. However, Elizabeth I did visit the site and it is rumoured that she rode her horse up the stairs.

The original manor of Salisbury Hall dates back to 1303 but the first mention of a hall was not until 1499 while a new manor house was built in the late sixteenth century. Most of the Salisbury Hall estate was sold off in 1904 for housing development and in 1952 the house was demolished.

In the 1950s a group of local volunteers undertook an archaeological excavation of the Salisbury Hall site before it was redeveloped. The excavation helped to understand the building's development and revealed the medieval foundations which aroused local interest in the site.

Castle House, Walthamstow, *c.* 1870. The Castle House, first occupied in 1800, became a popular landmark with the construction in 1829 of the Woodford New Road which ran past it.

In 1879 Castle House was destroyed by fire. A new house was quickly built and in 1887 when it was purchased by William McCall, a leading figure in Barnardo's, the house's name change to The Woodlands. Soon after his death in 1929 The Woodlands was demolished.

Belle Vue House, also known as Cook's Folly, Hale End Road, Walthamstow, *c.* 1910. The house was built by Charles Cook(e), a millionaire publisher, who died in 1816 after only a few years of enjoying his house. (His name is spelled differently in different records.) It was demolished in 1935.

Etloe House, Church Road, Leyton, April 1893. Built in about 1760 Etloe House was enlarged by the addition of two flanking wings in the early or mid-nineteenth century and at the same time the front was remodelled in a Tudor style. The most famous resident of this house was Cardinal Wiseman who moved there in 1856.

Residents of Bungalow Town, Lea Bridge Road, Leyton, in their garden, *c.* 1920. Just after the First World War a bungalow town developed near Seymour, Bloxhall and Perth Roads, off Lea Bridge Road. In most of the cases even though the houses were of poor quality, the gardens were well maintained with vegetables and flowers.

Nursery Cottages, Hitcham Road, Leyton in about 1930.

Nos 647–665 High Road, Leyton, 1901. This mix of house styles was soon to make way for a more standardized shop-fronted street.

Vine Cottage, James Lane, Leytonstone, 1896. As the area developed the rural nature of some of the streets disappeared.

The Blue Cottage, Blackhorse Lane, Walthamstow, *c.* 1900. Blackhorse Lane started to be developed at the beginning of the twentieth century in particular as a centre for light industry. The Blue Cottage was roughly where the junction of Blenheim Road and Blackhorse Lane is today.

Higham Hill Lodge, Blackhorse Lane, Walthamstow, *c.* 1890. The Lodge was built in about 1745 as a merchant's house. The site was left to decay during the twentieth century and was demolished in 1992; industrial units were built on the site in 1993.

Barclay House, Knotts Green, Leyton, *c.* 1895. Built in 1786 as Knotts Green House, it had a richly decorated interior with moulded panels and plaques. Gilbert Slater, an East India merchant, owned the house between 1786 and 1793 and in 1821 it was purchased by the Barclay family, the financiers, and became Barclay's House. In 1900 it became Livingstone Medical College for Missionaries.

In 1961 Livingstone Medical College was demolished and was replaced by Livingstone College Towers, shown here in 1964. In 1995 the tower was demolished and replaced by housing.

The Beaumont Road Estate, Leyton, under construction in 1965. Like other areas of Britain, Chingford, Leyton and Walthamstow underwent the development of high-rise flats and extensive council-run estates during the 1960s.

Oliver Close prefab bungalow estate, Leyton, viewed from the tower block on Leyton Grange Estate, 1961. The need for large estates came from an increasing population as well as a decline in the quality of temporary accommodation erected after 1945 for families displaced during the war.

Children playing cricket in the garden of a prefab house at the junction of Sinnott Road and Billet Road, Walthamstow, 1947. Life on the postwar prefab housing estates was fairly stark but they did provide what was assumed to be a temporary stop gap to more permanent homes.

Markhouse Avenue *c*. 1910. This road was first occupied in 1887 and shows how the streets of the area presently covered by Waltham Forest appeared to be fairly idyllic at the turn of the century; they were clean, car free and often tree lined.

Chingford Mount Road, Chingford, *c*. 1910.

CHAPTER SEVEN

SHOPPING & RETAILING

Rufus the prize-winning horse, c. 1895. Rufus was owned by J.E. Ball, a grocer who ran a shop on Lea Bridge Road, Leyton. This photograph was taken at the junction of Lowther Road and Goldsmith Road, Walthamstow and shows Mr Ball holding Rufus, two small boys who are William Ball and his brother, standing next to their uncle. On the right is the shop's errand boy.

The District Supply Stores at 1 High Street, Walthamstow, *c.* 1900. This style of open-fronted fruit and vegetable store was common in the borough at the turn of the century.

J. Clover butchers, 148 Wood Street, Walthamstow, *c.* 1895. In days gone by the butchers would hang their meat outside the shop and one can imagine how the street might have smelled.

The High Street, Walthamstow, 1907. The best-known shopping area in Waltham Forest is Walthamstow High Street which houses the market. The street, which is roughly a mile long, has also housed many of the country's top chain stores as well as family-run shops.

The High Street, Walthamstow, between the junctions of Pretoria Avenue and Carisbrooke Road, 1957. During the market the area becomes a hive of activity. The market was first held in 1885 and in 1932 stallholders became licensed to prevent squabbles over plots and also to pay for cleaning of the High Street.

Earp's Cash Stores, Blackhorse Road, Walthamstow, *c.* 1910. Many shop owners took pride in their property and would have impressive window displays to show what was on sale.

Louis Green's sweet shop at 276 Church Road, Leyton, 1957. This shop was very popular with the local children for obvious reasons. In the photograph are the proprietor and assistant.

R.W. Pettit & Son of High Street, Walthamstow, delivered milk throughout the borough as shown by this delivery cart in Leyton, 1917. The milk was carried in a churn on the cart and then poured out at the doorstep. At the time of this photograph women had taken over the role of delivering the milk as many of the young men had been called up to fight in the First World War.

Construction of shops and flats on Forest Road, Walthamstow, 1924. With the limits on space when shops were built, a flat would be included above, often for the shop owner or employee.

The Avenue, Higham's Park, 1920s. Before the introduction of the motor vehicle delivery was by cart or bicycle like the one outside Hollingshead and Upson, wine merchants.

Church Lane, Leytonstone in 1876. Among the private houses on the left is a shop selling tea and coffee. This is reminiscent of a village scene but is in fact just off the High Road, Leytonstone.

The junction of High Road and Church Lane, Leytonstone, 1932. This building housed the *Independent* newspaper office on the ground floor.

Hoe Street, Walthamstow, from the railway bridge, looking north, *c.* 1910.

Hoe Street, Walthamstow, from the railway bridge, looking north, 1972. Some scenes have changed very little as can be seen from the two images on this page. The Tower Hotel, now the Goose and Granite, dominates the corner of Hoe Street and Selbourne Road while the trams have been replaced by buses. However, if the planners had got their way in 1948 all these shops would have been demolished for a purpose-built shopping arcade.

This 1920s photograph shows the cobbler's on Church Lane, Walthamstow, and its owner, Mr Welsh, is standing in front of the fence.

High Road, Leyton, near the Midland Station, June 1905. On the left is a barber's and the barber, probably Burt William the owner, watches as his neighbour, John H. Rumble the butcher takes a delivery.

A book and confectionery stall on the east side of Blue Row, Leyton High Road, *c.* 1907.

W. Laver's Laundry on the Blue Row, Leyton High Road, 1898. Monday was the typical wash day but while women carried out these tasks at home, in the laundries men were in charge of a predominately female workforce.

CHAPTER EIGHT

LEISURE & ENTERTAINMENT

The Bell public house, at the junction of Forest Road and Chingford Road, Walthamstow, c. 1910. Many locals spent their leisure time in the public houses. During the Victorian era many were built or extended to cater for the increasing population. The original Bell public house was built in 1857 and was then rebuilt in 1900.

The King's Head Hotel, King's Head Hill, Chingford, *c.* 1900.

The Three Blackbirds public house, High Road, Leyton, in 1876 prior to the rebuilding. This pub existed by 1705 and has survived all the developments that have taken place around it although it underwent rebuilding in about 1876 to cater for increased trade.

The Royal Forest Hotel, Ranger's Road, Chingford, *c*. 1910. The Royal Forest Hotel was built in 1880 to cater for daytrippers brought to the area by the construction of the railway line to Chingford in 1873 and The Epping Forest Act, 1878, which guaranteed its preservation as an open space for the population.

The Royal Forest Hotel almost came to an untimely end in 1912. A fire swept through the building and the Chingford Volunteer Fire Brigade fought the blaze. On the following day locals came to view the clearing up.

Some leisure time was used for raising money for charities. In about 1910 a football match took place between the 'top hats' and 'bonnets' in Lloyd Park to raise funds for the construction of a new ambulance station in Walthamstow.

The Walthamstow Palace Theatre dominating the High Street, Walthamstow, 1920s. On 28 December 1903 the Palace Theatre opened and became the most recognisable leisure building in the borough. Topping the bill on the opening night was the Fred Karnos Company in a programme called *Jailbirds*. The Palace gave its last performance in 1954 and was demolished in 1960.

Walthamstow Stadium, Chingford Road, Chingford, 1960s. This stadium, opened in 1931, was once in Walthamstow but with boundary changes it 'moved' to Chingford. The familiar frontage, lit up by neon lights at night, was used in local band East 17's video 'House of Love' (1993).

Queuing outside the Granada cinema, Hoe Street, Walthamstow for tickets for a Beatles concert, Sunday 28 June 1964. The Granada cinema opened on the 15 September 1930 and was also used for live shows. It is now the ABC cinema.

The bathing pool at Whipps Cross under construction in May 1907. From the beginning of the twentieth century swimming became a growing leisure pursuit and to meet the demand outdoor pools were built, such as the one at Whipps Cross which was excavated by the unemployed of Leyton. This pool was converted into a bathing lake in 1932 and in 1937 to a modern open-air pool, the Whipps Cross Lido.

The Whipps Cross Lido, Whipps Cross Road, Leytonstone, June 1960. This pool remained a popular attraction in the 1960s and 1970s but after further leisure venues were built in the borough and interest in swimming waned the pool was closed and demolished in 1983.

The impressive entrance at Cathall Road Swimming Baths, Leytonstone, 1902. Cathall Road Baths were opened in 1902 and in 1931 a public wash-house was added. Today a swimming baths and a leisure centre are on this site.

The top end of the High Street, Walthamstow showing the Central Library and swimming baths in 1910. Often leisure facilities are located together and in 1900 swimming baths were built between the Central Library and Monoux Grammar School which meant library users and visitors to the High Street market could also go swimming. The baths were demolished in 1968.

Leyton Ladies Band, 1890s. Like elsewhere in the country most leisure activities were aimed at men. Women had to find their own ways of using their free time, albeit within the limitations of having to look after children and home. Little is known about this ladies band but this image clearly shows how women provided their own entertainment.

Essex v. Middlesex during the Leyton Cricket Week, 31 July 1957. Essex County Cricket Club played on Lyttleton Ground, Leyton High Road, between 1885 and 1933. In 1932 the Yorkshire openers Holmes and Sutcliffe made a record breaking first wicket stand of 555 against Essex on this ground. In 1957 The Essex Cricket Week was re-established.

Carnivals were often the highlight of the summer. However, not all went without a hitch. During the Leyton Carnival of 1933 the Carnival Queen's float got stuck under the railway bridge on Grove Green Road, Leytonstone. The crowds are seen watching as efforts are made to free the float. In this year Miss May Knight was the Carnival Queen.

The Leyton Borough Show, 1952. Children looked forward to the arrival of the circus or fair and in Leyton the Borough Show provided a range of rides and attractions like this roundabout.

Councillor A.W. Golightly laying the foundation stone for the Lea Bridge Road Branch Library, 30 September 1905. At the turn of the twentieth century local governments tried to show civic pride through the provision of sports and educational facilities. Leyton Urban District Council sought suitable locations for branch libraries and this one, funded by a donation from the Carnegie Trust, opened to the public in 1906.

Walthamstow Central Library opened on the High Street in 1894. In 1907 the lending library, designed by J.W. Dunford, was constructed with a donation of £10,000 from the Carnegie Trust.

After refurbishment the Leyton Central Lending Library was reopened on 1 September 1929 by the Mayor of Leyton, Alderman W.C. Russell. The poet and playwright, John Drinkwater (1883–1937) who was born on Fairlop Road, Leytonstone, is standing to the left of the mayor.

Vestry House, Vestry Road, Walthamstow, 1870s. In 1931 the Walthamstow Museum opened in the newly converted workhouse and in 1933 the council acquired the remaining part of the building. In 1965 Walthamstow Museum became the borough's museum and later changed its name to Vestry House Museum.

The Walthamstow Museum was opened on 2 May 1931 by the Right Honourable Lord Hanworth, KBE, Master of the Rolls who also opened the museum extension on 3 February 1934.

Water House, Forest Road, Walthamstow, 1908. William Morris was born at Elm House, Forest Road on 24 March 1834 and in 1840 his family moved to Woodford Hall. With the death of his father in 1847 the family moved back to Walthamstow and lived in the Water House from 1848 to 1857. The house was then purchased by Edward Lloyd, the newspaper publisher, after whom Lloyd Park is named.

In 1950 the William Morris Gallery, Forest Road, Walthamstow was opened by Clement Attlee, MP for Walthamstow West (1950–6). In 1951 Queen Mary visited the gallery, shown above. She had had a long-standing relationship with Morris and Company and the firm made items for her wedding.

Queen Elizabeth's Hunting Lodge, Ranger's Road, Chingford, *c*. 1900. The building was opened to the public as the Epping Forest Museum in 1895. It was ideally suited for visitors to Epping Forest and originally contained exhibitions about life in Epping Forest. The building itself underwent restoration during 1899 to 1900 and during the early 1990s. After the latter work the museum reopened to the public in 1993.

The Museum Room at the White House, Leyton Green Road, 1927. Private individuals also built up collections and developed their own museums in their homes.

CHAPTER NINE

PARKS & OPEN SPACES

The Marsh Gate to Markhouse Common, Walthamstow, 1860. This gate was at the present junction of St James's Street and Station Road and this view is looking up St James's Street with the Coach and Horses public house on the right corner. Access to the marsh land was restricted by the Marsh Gates which were intended to prevent animals from straying. The Marshlands remained common ground until large parts were purchased and developed by the East London Water Co. between 1853 and 1904.

Friday Hill, looking down Simmons Lane, Chingford, 1930s. Well into the twentieth century large parts of Chingford remained rural in appearance and even today around one quarter of Chingford is still green. This view shows the lack of housing development and explains why people came here for calm and quiet.

Entrance to Ainslie Wood, Chingford, *c.* 1910. All around modern-day Waltham Forest are small wooded areas, many of which run into Epping Forest.

Whipps Cross Road, Leytonstone, *c.* 1898. In Leytonstone much of the green space has been lost to housing development and in this view the trees hide the fact that just out of camera range houses had already been built. Even so the east side of the road was open space as it is today and made a perfect place for a lazy afternoon outing.

The boat house at Whipps Cross Pond, Leytonstone, *c.* 1915. Whipps Cross Pond has been a magnet for children and adults for almost 100 years and is still popular for fishing, walking and boating.

Higham's Park Lake, Chingford, June 1904. Higham Hall was built in 1768 and in 1793 the garden designer, Humphry Repton, was employed to landscape the land. Higham's Park evolved from this land and Repton's lake still exists as a focal point.

A family stop off to taste the blackberries while out for a leisurely stroll in Higham's Park, Chingford, c. 1910. At the turn of the century the developing parks became popular for family walks as well as sometimes for collecting the wild fruits.

Lloyd Park, Forest Road, Walthamstow, during its public opening by Sam Wood MP, 1900. Where large parts of the forest had been removed, parks opened up either on wasteland or on land which had once been the gardens of the large houses. Lloyd Park developed from the grounds of Lloyd House, now the William Morris Gallery. The bandstand was in the lower field and the Sunday concerts were held there.

Lloyd Park, Forest Road, Walthamstow, c. 1910. The upper part of Lloyd Park contained the formally laid out gardens. The pillar top seen in this image was donated to the borough by Mr Frank Mortimer, a local stone mason who had purchased it from the recently demolished general post office at St Martin-le-Grand in the City of London. Locals appear to have disagreed about its suitability for Lloyd Park for several years and in 1954 it was transferred to Vestry Road where it can still be seen today.

The entrance to Larkswood, Chingford, *c.* 1910. Chingford was relatively late in feeling the effects of the spread of housing and large areas of woodland and open space still remain today. Here a group of women take a take a leisurely stroll.

Moon Farm, Billet Road, Walthamstow, 1920s. This land was purchased by George Monoux in 1507 and appears to have had a farm on it from then until 1927 when Warner Estates developed the land for housing. The farmhouse shown above was built in about 1701 and was pulled down in 1927.

With farming came risks. The commonest of these was straying animals but also at harvest time fire could present a major problem. In 1908 this haystack in Chingford caught fire and onlookers watched as the volunteers fought to save the haystack but it must be assumed that with such poor equipment it would have been a losing battle.

Pimp Hall Farm, Chingford, *c.* 1900. Apart from the woods and parks, the final remaining open spaces in the borough were the farms. The sixteenth-century farmhouse was demolished in the 1930s, the barn fell down in 1990 but the sixteenth-century dovecote (left) still stands and the plan of the farmhouse is marked on the ground on the site today.

Low Hall Farm, Walthamstow, *c.* 1930. During the seventeenth century a smaller building was constructed on top of the old Low Hall Manor House which dated from the fourteenth century and had fallen into decay. The building pictured used some of the earlier foundations and various alterations took place in the eighteenth century. By the nineteenth century the building declined to the status of farmhouse. In August 1944 the farmhouse was destroyed by a flying bomb which landed on the fountain. Archaeological excavation work on the site in 1997, prior to housing development, uncovered the sequences of building development from the fourteenth century to modern day and even found remnants of the flying bomb.

Ruckholt Farm, Leyton, *c.* 1900. Like the Low Hall site, Ruckholt Manor, first recorded in the sixteenth century, eventually declined. It was demolished between 1755 and 1757 and the materials were sold. A farmhouse was in existence on the Ruckholt Manor land by 1777 with farm buildings lying just south of the site of the manor house, and the farm covered about 180 acres.

CHAPTER TEN

WAR

The last group of the Local Volunteers was photographed outside the Drill Hall, Church Hill Road, Walthamstow, in 1907. Many of these young men went off seeking adventure but fell prey to illness or death even before seeing any fighting.

War had a major impact on the local population. Volunteers from the area appear to have served in all of the Victorian and twentieth century campaigns. On 17 November 1900 celebrations for the returning City Imperial Volunteers from South Africa were held at the Drill Hall on Church Hill, Walthamstow. Sergeant Finch is seen here waiting to serve drinks.

Celebrations at the Drill Hall, Church Hill, Walthamstow, for the returning City Imperial Volunteers, 17 November 1900.

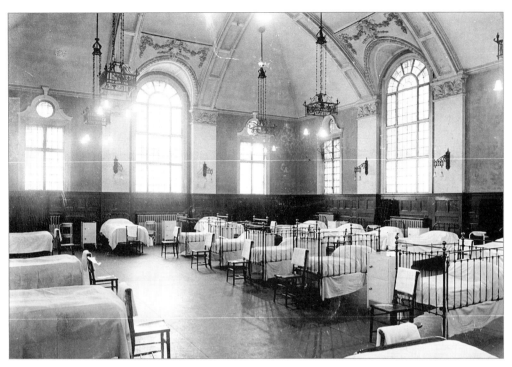

The First World War was the first time that conflict overseas directly affected the local population. The risk of bombings from airships increased as the war went on and the vast numbers of wounded soldiers returning meant that some local buildings were adapted to serve as hospitals. One such building was the Central Library, High Street, Walthamstow, but it was never used for the purpose.

Various fund-raising events took place throughout Chingford, Leyton and Walthamstow to pay for equipment and to raise awareness of the machinery in use during the First World War. One such event was the Walthamstow Tank Day, 9 March 1918 at Selbourne Park, Walthamstow.

Leyton Emergency Corps carries out training in 1918. With the threat of German air attack on London, emergency corps were set up to help in the rescue and treatment of injured civilians.

Richard's Place, Walthamstow, 1918. Various parts of the borough were damaged in airship raids. The damage caused by the bombs, totalling around 1,300 houses in Leyton, was much less than was to follow in the next war but even so it shocked people to realise how vulnerable they were.

No. 33 Rensbury Road, Walthamstow, 1919. The cease-fire was called in November 1918 but it was not until the signing of the peace terms in 1919 that local residents could at last mark the end of the war. Peace parties were held throughout the country with many houses and streets being decorated.

Peace party on Luton Road, Walthamstow, 1919. In many streets peace parties included the preparation of a large meal with all the local children being invited.

The First World War had seen many young lives lost in the name of peace. On 15 July 1922 the cenotaph on Forest Road, Walthamstow, was unveiled. This memorial was moved up Forest Road to the gardens of the town hall in November 1961.

During the early 1930s a mood of gloom spread throughout Europe with the realization that Hitler appeared to be intent on dragging Europe back into war. It was clear that the civilian population would be targeted but unfortunately with the International Crisis of September 1938 the precautions seemed inadequate, as shown by these hastily excavated trenches on Oliver Road, Leyton.

Surface public air-raid shelter, Whipps Cross Road, Leyton, 1942. By the time the war was at its height civilian shelters had improved. This type of shelter was the standard style. The white paint lines on it and the bus shelter were intended to make them visible to vehicles during the black-out.

Many photographs show the interiors of these surface shelters as being very hospitable, like this one on Chingford Green. Unfortunately this was not necessarily the case. They were prone to flooding, became overcrowded, were often damp and cold, and provided no privacy.

Warden's post at Green Man Pond, Leytonstone, *c.* 1942. Civil Defence wardens were much maligned at the start of the war. During the phoney war, September 1939 to May 1940, many civilians objected to their officious manner. However, by the end of the war the public had only admiration for these men and women who risked their lives to save others.

Civil Defence stores at Larkswood, *c.* 1945. The Civil Defence was also expected to have sufficient equipment and supplies to maintain their service and these stores at Larkswood provided equipment needed by the Chingford ARP.

The army's bomb disposal units were kept very busy. They were called to St Peter's Avenue, Walthamstow, where this bomb fell on the 24 September 1940. Once made safe some of these bombs would then be displayed for propaganda. During the Second World War excluding the V1 and V2 attacks there were 370 incidents in Chingford, 765 in Leyton and 776 in Walthamstow.

Clearing up after the V2 attack on Endlebury Road, Chingford, 5 February 1945. As the war went on more destructive weapons were developed. Londoners felt that because Allied forces had landed in France they would be safe from bombing but soon the reprisal weapons, the V1s and V2s, started. Chingford was hit by 11 V1s and 11 V2s, Leyton was hit by 28 V1s, and 11 V2s, while Walthamstow was hit by 17 V1s and 15 V2s.

Fire-fighting unit at ASEA, Fulbourne Road, Walthamstow, *c.* 1945. Local companies set up their own civil defence units with many developing from existing units such as at ASEA, which produced electric motors and transformers.

Lea Hall Road Fire-Fighters, Leyton, *c.* 1942. During the heavy months of the Blitz residential areas were overlooked because factories were deemed more important to save. The government issued instructions on how to help put out fires and many residential streets set up volunteer fire-fighting units made up of local residents.

Children on Wood Street, Walthamstow, during War Weapons Week, May 1941. During the war special events took place to raise funds for the forces and also to boost public morale.

A Christmas party for children of Allied prisoners of war from Leyton, Leyton town hall, 23 December 1944. Where possible the local authorities tried to make life as normal as possible. This party was hosted by Mayor Rayner of Leyton.

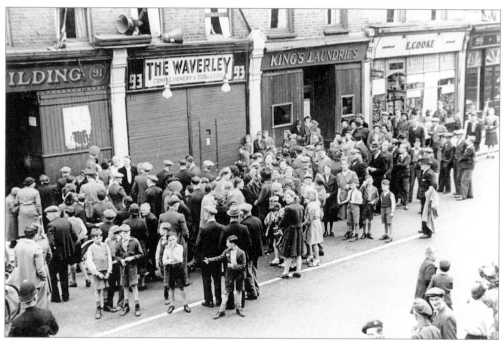

The announcement of peace in Europe made by Winston Churchill is broadcast to the waiting crowds outside The Waverley, 93 Wood Street, Walthamstow, 3 p.m. 8 May 1945. Mr A.J. Symons, the owner of the Waverley, kept a photographic record of events in the Wood Street area during the war.

Thanksgiving celebrations at Leyton Orient Football Club, Brisbane Road, Leyton, 1945. At the end of the war peace celebrations took place throughout the borough. The usual street parties were most common but there was also a series of larger thanksgiving events.

CHAPTER ELEVEN

MADE IN WALTHAM FOREST

Alf and Fred Bremer sitting in their early motor car with Tom Bates standing next to it, Grosvenor Park Road, Walthamstow, c. 1918. Frederick Bremer (1872–1941) was one of Britain's motor car pioneers. Along with Tom Bates, he constructed a vehicle with an internal combustion engine between 1892 and 1894 which was recognized as the first British-built motor car during a debate in 1912 held by the Motor Magazine. *The car was built at 1 Connaught Road, Walthamstow. After a short spell living at Albert Road, Frederick Bremer moved to 27 Grosvenor Park Road and from there Bremer and Bates ran an engineering company, listed between 1912 and 1926 but probably surviving into the 1930s.*

A.V. Roe (1877–1958) was one of Britain's air pioneers. In 1909 on Walthamstow Marshes he carried out the first flight in an all-British aircraft – prior to this the engines had been made overseas – and he went on to found the Avro company famed for its Second World War bombers. (Photograph reproduced by kind permission of the Science Museum London/Science & Society Picture Library)

Steven's Coach Builders, Budds Alley, Wood Street, Walthamstow, c. 1900. As the borough was fairly rural in parts up until the late Victorian era countryside crafts still flourished, including coach building.

Coach builders had to adapt to the introduction of motorized vehicles. Abbott's Cart Builders, Colchester Road, Walthamstow, founded in 1893, started out producing hand- and horse-drawn carts for bakers, dairies and laundries. The firm eventually started to produce bodies for motorized vehicles, such as this 1920s van produced for Ensigns, a local camera company based at Fulbourne Road, Walthamstow.

During the First World War Wrighton Furniture Manufacturers produced crutches for disabled servicemen but during the Second World War it had the bigger task of producing the bodywork for the wooden Mosquito aircraft. It is surprising that this photograph was taken because it dates from a period of major wartime restriction on the publication of information and we can see the company's name, location and date of photograph included.

Studio Populaire, Forest Road, Walthamstow, 1950s. Before cameras became accessible to the masses, studios produced portraits and by the 1930s were branching out into supplying equipment and specializing in photographing events such as parties and weddings. This studio was run by Dickie Jackson and many of his photographs are held by Vestry House Museum.

Leyton and Leytonstone Volunteer Fire Brigade being filmed for the British and Colonial film *While London Sleeps*, 1914. Several major film studios were based in Walthamstow including Broadwest Film Company at 245 Wood Street (1916–24) and British and Colonial Film Company at 317–19 Hoe Street (1913–24).

Collier Brothers Brewery, St James Street, Walthamstow, 1880s. William Hawes built the steam-powered Walthamstow Brewery in St James Street in about 1859 and in 1871 the Essex Brewery Co. Ltd was formed to buy the brewery. Their venture failed, however, and the brewery was acquired by Collier Brothers who operated it as the Essex Brewery until 1922 when Tollemache's Breweries Ltd purchased it and ran it until it closed in 1971.

West's Brewery depot, 272–284 Grove Green Road, Leytonstone, c. 1925.

Buck's Bakery, 568 High Road, Leytonstone, *c.* 1905. Joseph Buck took over the Elms Bakery in 1905 and the shop remained in the Buck family for several generations.

Monster Christmas Cake, 1913. Buck's became famous for its huge Christmas cakes that went in the shop window over the festive season. These were started by Joseph Buck who liked to model them on historic buildings and, even though he was of German descent, often produced buildings related to the British royal family, as in this example depicting Buckingham Palace. The cakes were continued by his son Frank who preferred to base his designs on buildings related to fairy stories.

Albion Bakery, Beulah Road, Walthamstow, *c.* 1905. This bakery was owned by William Thomas and we can see the delivery boy ready for his local rounds with bread in basket, while the further afield deliveries are about to be made by the horse and cart.

Delivery man Ernest Barker and a boy from Day's and Sons Bakery, Higham Hill Road, Walthamstow, 1920s. This style of hand delivery cart was typical well into the twentieth century but we can imagine how hard it would have been to push it up the steep local roads.

Hitchman's Dairies factory, North Circular Road, Walthamstow, *c.* 1970. Hitchman's was founded in the 1880s and moved to the North Circular Road in 1939. In 1963 it joined United Dairies and started to produce fruit juice in 1974. Fresh milk production ceased in 1982 and the plant was transferred to St Ivel. It closed down in 1992/3.

During the First World War many of the typically male dominated jobs were taken over by women. Farmers & Cleveland Dairies Co. Ltd was located at 203 Hoe Street and 178 Forest Road, Walthamstow. In this 1916 staff photograph are three sisters: Vera (front left), Ella (front second left) and Honor (middle front) Neale. Vera Neale operated the Hoe Street to Wood Street delivery run.

Manual production of condoms at London Rubber Company (LRC), North Circular Road, Chingford, 1941. Manual production ceased in the 1950s with the introduction of automatic plants, designed by LRC, and first installed in 1951. While in Waltham Forest LRC became the world's largest condom manufacturer as well as producing other protectives, household and surgeons' gloves.

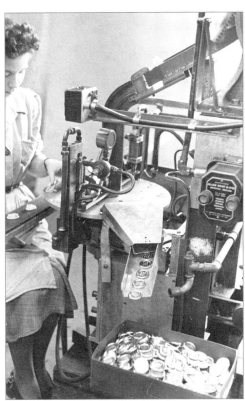

Packaging of diaphragms at the LRC, North Circular Road, Chingford, c. 1950. One of the borough's largest employers and worldwide known company, LRC moved to Chingford in 1937 and remained there until 1994 when it transferred to Broxbourne.

Pettit and Son's pottery, Folly Lane, Higham Hill, *c.* 1890s. This company was founded in 1868 by William Pettit and produced unglazed pots, saucers and chimney pots, until 1944. When the tomato industry developed in Lea Valley, production changed to flower pots.

Staff of Edward Roe, a builder and plumber on Cann Hall Road, Leyton, are ready to depart from outside the shop, 1908. Many employers realized that the pressures on their staff were quite high and to create better working relationships between the management and workers annual outings were organized.

Mr Breeden shaping the face of a cricket bat with a draw knife in his workshop on High Road, Leyton, *c*. 1920. Many small industries relied on the individual skills of the owner. Breeden's was set up in by 1874 by William James Breeden and survived as a family business until 1984.

Delivery vehicles for London Electric Wire Company and Smiths Limited (LEWCOS), Church Road, Leyton. This firm moved to Leyton in 1899 and produced electric cables, wire and flex. By the 1960s it was one of the largest employers in Leyton and the largest manufacturer of insulated wire in Europe. In about 1994 the company, then HES Optics, ceased trading.

Barnet Ensign Ross Ltd, Fulbourne Road, Walthamstow, *c.* 1948. The Houghton-Butcher story is one of amalgamation and the association of companies to boost sales of photographic equipment and consolidate a market position. After various name changes in 1948 it became Barnet Ensign Ross Ltd. The company moved to Clapham in 1954.

Staff arriving at the British Xylonite Factory, Larkshall Road, Hale End, July 1908. British Xylonite was the first large company to move into Walthamstow, opening a factory in 1897. It pioneered the manufacture of celluloid in Britain and in 1939 the Hale End Works, under the name of Halex Ltd. became the centre of production of the group's plastic goods such as combs and toothbrushes.

Walthamstow Mill in Coppermill Lane has undergone many changes. Originally a paper-mill in 1653 it has had other uses including the manufacture of leather and linseed oil. In 1808 the mill was purchased by the British Copper Co. to roll copper, and copper tokens were struck here in the mint. In 1860 it was purchased by the East London Waterworks Co. and converted into a pumping station.

Associated Fire Alarms Ltd, Claremont Road, Walthamstow, 1964. This company produced fire and burglar alarms, and was based in Sutherland Road between 1920 and the 1950s before moving to Claremont Road and then to Billet Road in 1961.

Wells Brimtoy, Stirling Road, Walthamstow, 1940s. A. Wells & Co. Ltd, toy manufacturers, moved to Somers Road, Walthamstow, in 1924 and in 1932 became known as Wells-Brimtoy Distributors Ltd. In 1938 the company moved to Stirling Road and in 1965 moved to Wales.

City Knitwear Ltd, Lea Bridge Road, Leyton, 1957. This company moved to Leyton in 1932 and produced ladies' and children's knitwear. All fabrics and garments were made on the site, the only outside work being the dyeing. In 1957 the company employed 160 staff at the factory and 300 to 400 outworkers.

R.A. Rooney and Sons Ltd, Higham Hill Road, *c*. 1905. This firm moved to the borough in 1901 and enlarged its premises in 1920. They manufacture a wide range of brushes including for teeth, shaving, hair, paint, toilet and floor cleaning.

ACKNOWLEDGEMENTS

This book would not have been possible without the support that the Waltham Forest museum and library services have received from the many residents of Chingford, Leyton and Walthamstow who have donated photographs. The Vestry House Museum collection has also relied heavily on the support and donations from local companies, especially the local *Guardian* newspaper, as well as the Chingford Historical Society, Walthamstow Historical Society, Waltham Forest Civic Society, Waltham Forest in Focus and Waltham Forest Oral History Workshop. I would also like to thank the Museum staff – Neil Bhupsingh, Victoria Coxon, Gary Heales and Linda Weston – the Local Studies Librarian Brian Mardall and the Borough Archivist Jo Parker for their assistance during the production of this publication and their dedication to preserving and interpreting local history.

Finally I must thank my parents for giving me my interest in history and Jackie Mulligan for her support during the research for this publication.

INDEX